IT'S TIME TO EAT PERSIMMON FRUIT

It's Time to Eat PERSIMMON FRUIT

Walter the Educator

Silent King Books
A WhichHead Entertainment Imprint

Copyright © 2024 by Walter the Educator

All rights reserved. No part of this book may be reproduced in any manner whatsoever without written per- mission except in the case of brief quotations embodied in critical articles and reviews.

First Printing, 2024

Disclaimer

This book is a literary work; the story is not about specific persons, locations, situations, and/or circumstances unless mentioned in a historical context. Any resemblance to real persons, locations, situations, and/or circumstances is coincidental. This book is for entertainment and informational purposes only. The author and publisher offer this information without warranties expressed or implied. No matter the grounds, neither the author nor the publisher will be accountable for any losses, injuries, or other damages caused by the reader's use of this book. The use of this book acknowledges an understanding and acceptance of this disclaimer.

It's Time to Eat PERSIMMON FRUIT is a collectible early learning book by Walter the Educator suitable for all ages belonging to Walter the Educator's Time to Eat Book Series. Collect more books at WaltertheEducator.com

USE THE EXTRA SPACE TO TAKE NOTES AND DOCUMENT YOUR MEMORIES

PERSIMMON FRUIT

The leaves are turning, red and gold,

It's Time to Eat
Persimmon Fruit

The air is crisp, the wind is cold.

It's time to pick a treat so sweet,

Persimmons ripe, a tasty feat!

Orange and round, they shine so bright,

Hanging in trees, a lovely sight.

Pluck them gently, don't let them fall,

The sweetest fruit is worth it all.

Wash them clean and take a bite,

A burst of flavor, pure delight.

Soft as honey, smooth and sweet,

Persimmons make the best fall treat.

Some are firm, you crunch and chew,

Others are soft, like pudding too!

Each one is special, ripe and fine,

A treasure of the autumn time.

It's Time to Eat
Persimmon Fruit

"Mommy, Daddy, come and see,

This persimmon's just for me!"

Little hands hold tight with care,

Juicy bites are everywhere.

Grandma says, "Now don't forget,

If it's still green, it's not ripe yet."

Wait until it's soft and bright,

That's when they're perfect, just right!

Sliced in circles, golden rings,

Persimmons make my heart just sing.

On pancakes, toast, or in a pie,

Persimmons make a happy sigh.

Birds love them too, they peck and munch,

They gather round for a fruity lunch.

But don't you worry, there's plenty here,

It's Time to Eat
Persimmon Fruit

Persimmons come each autumn year!

Let's share this treat with friends today,

There's more than enough to give away.

A fruit so sweet, it's made to share,

Persimmons show we truly care.

The season's short, it won't last long,

Soon persimmon time will be gone.

So let's enjoy each bite, so sweet,

It's Time to Eat
Persimmon Fruit

Hooray for persimmons, what a treat!

ABOUT THE CREATOR

Walter the Educator is one of the pseudonyms for Walter Anderson. Formally educated in Chemistry, Business, and Education, he is an educator, an author, a diverse entrepreneur, and he is the son of a disabled war veteran. "Walter the Educator" shares his time between educating and creating. He holds interests and owns several creative projects that entertain, enlighten, enhance, and educate, hoping to inspire and motivate you. Follow, find new works, and stay up to date with Walter the Educator™

at WaltertheEducator.com

www.ingramcontent.com/pod-product-compliance
Lightning Source LLC
LaVergne TN
LVHW052014060526
838201LV00059B/4022